THiS BOOK BELONGS

....

COLOR TEST PAGE

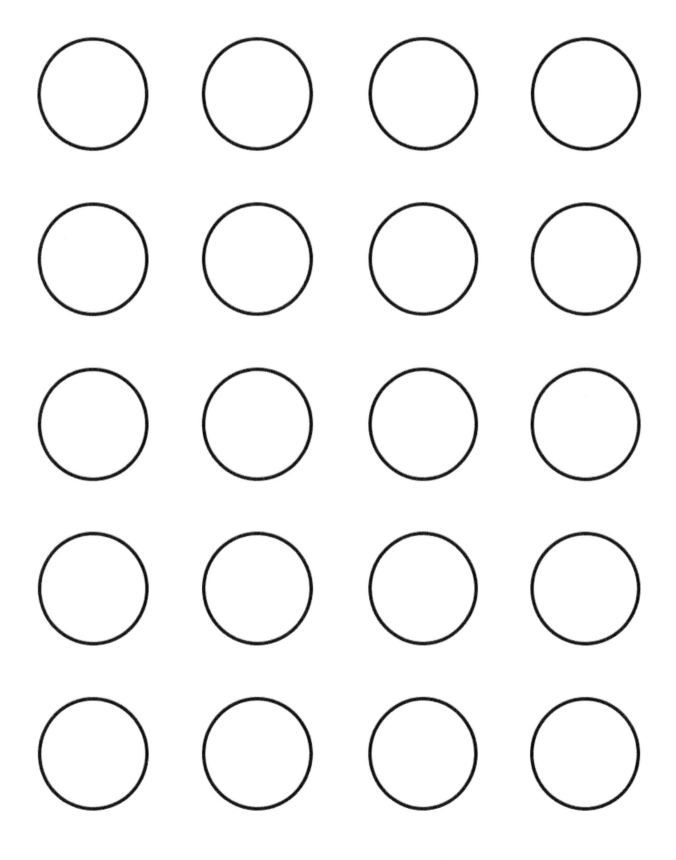

A FRIEND WITH WEED IS A FRIEND INDEED

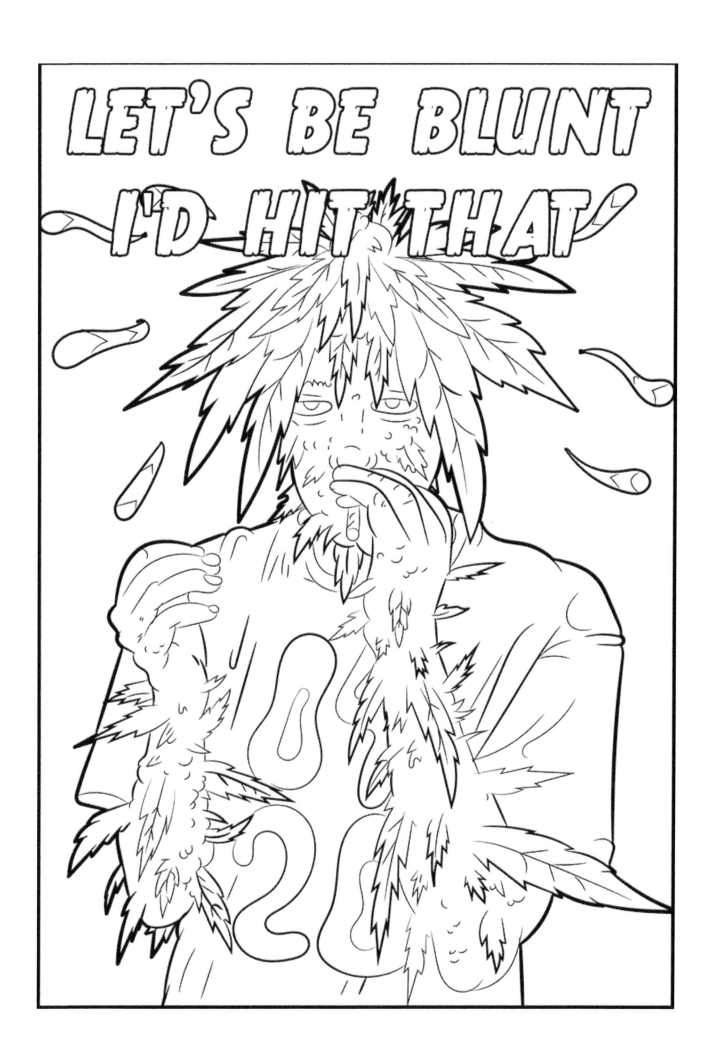

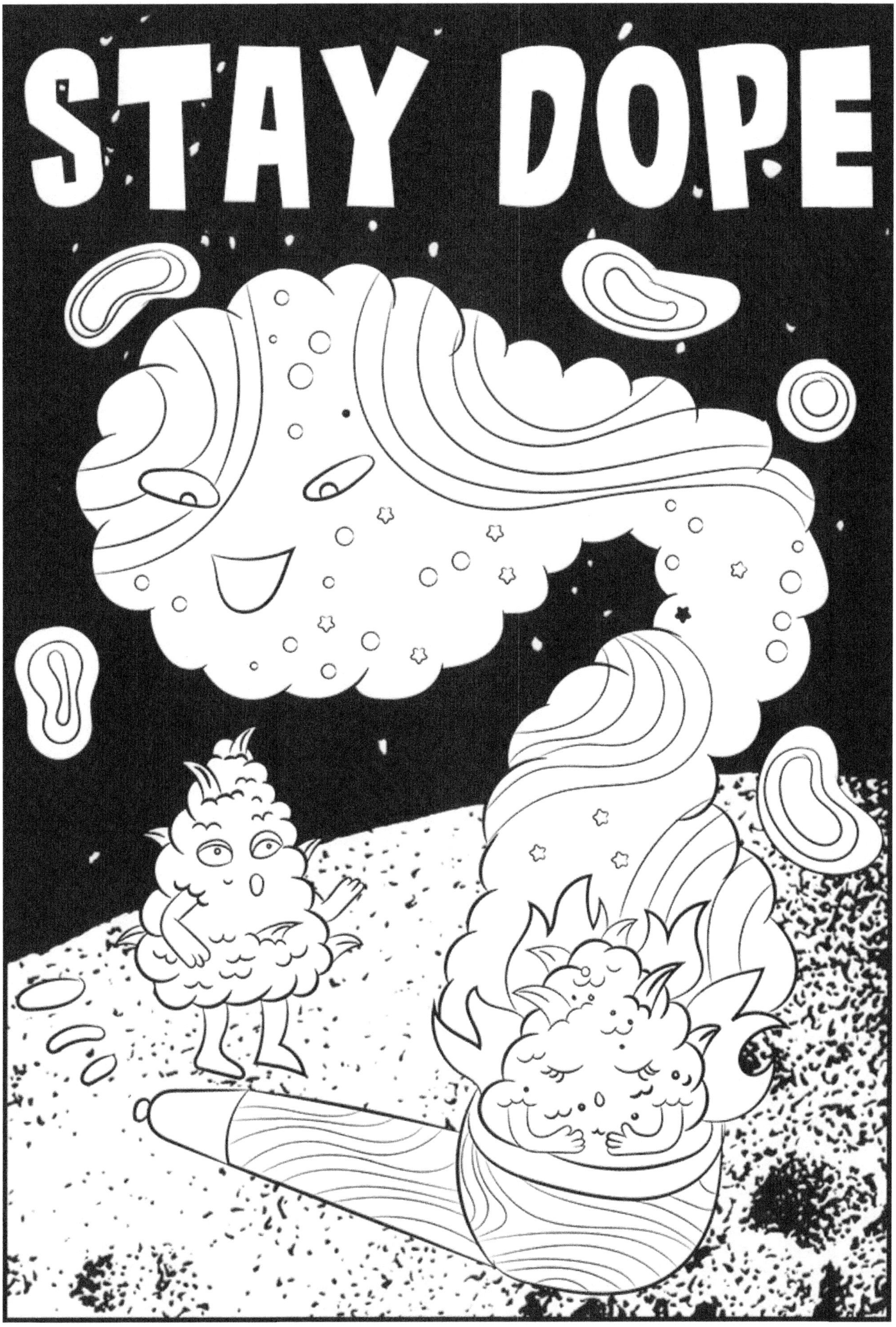
STAY DOPE

PIZZA & WEED IS ALL I NEED

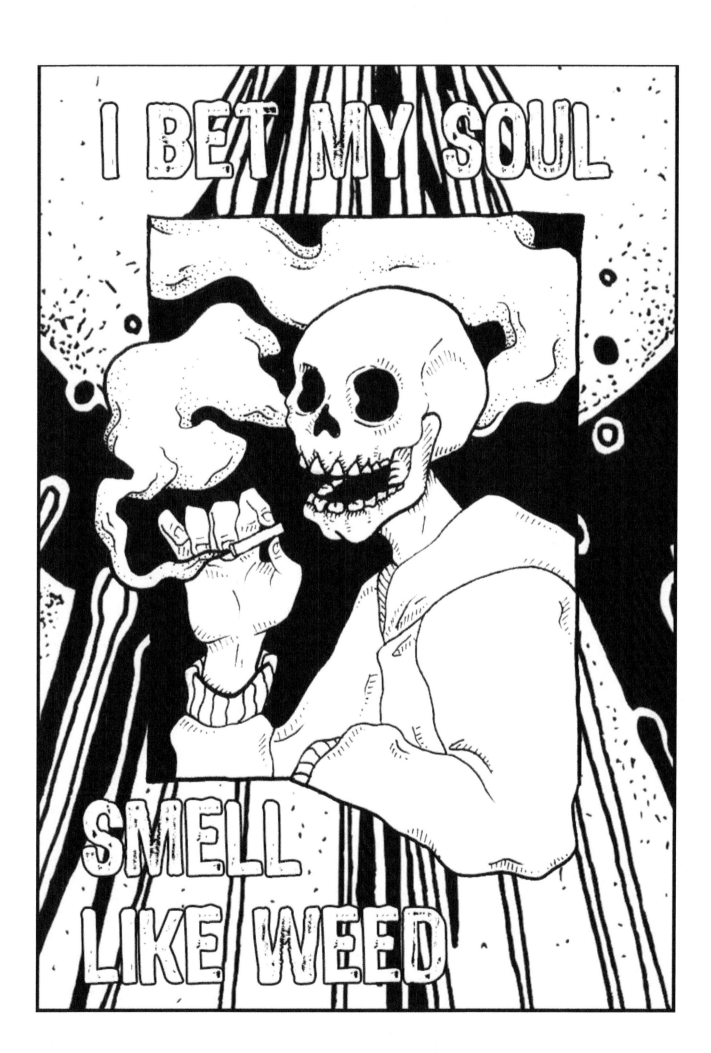

HIGH AS A KITE

WEDDING CAKE

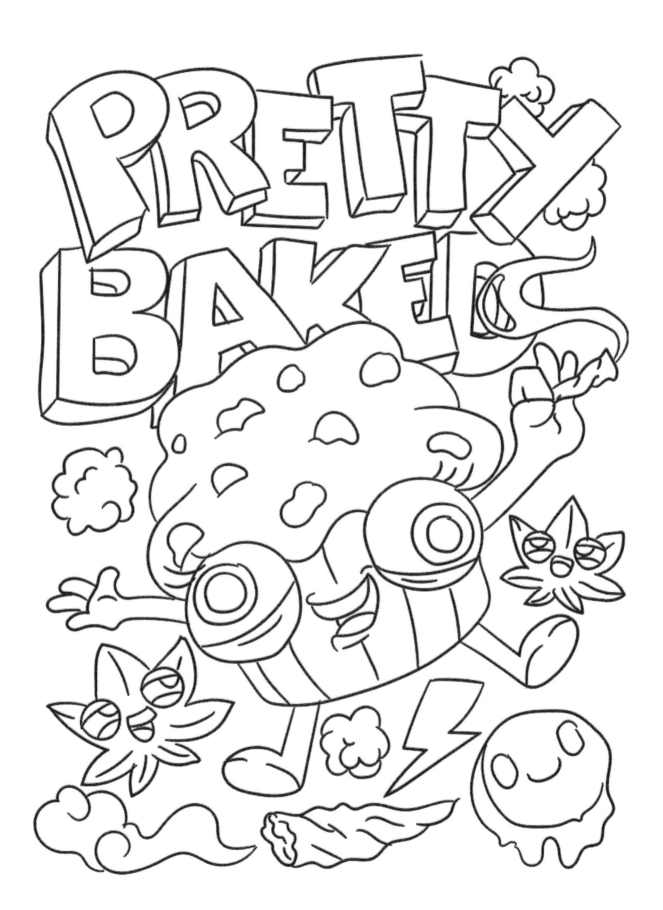

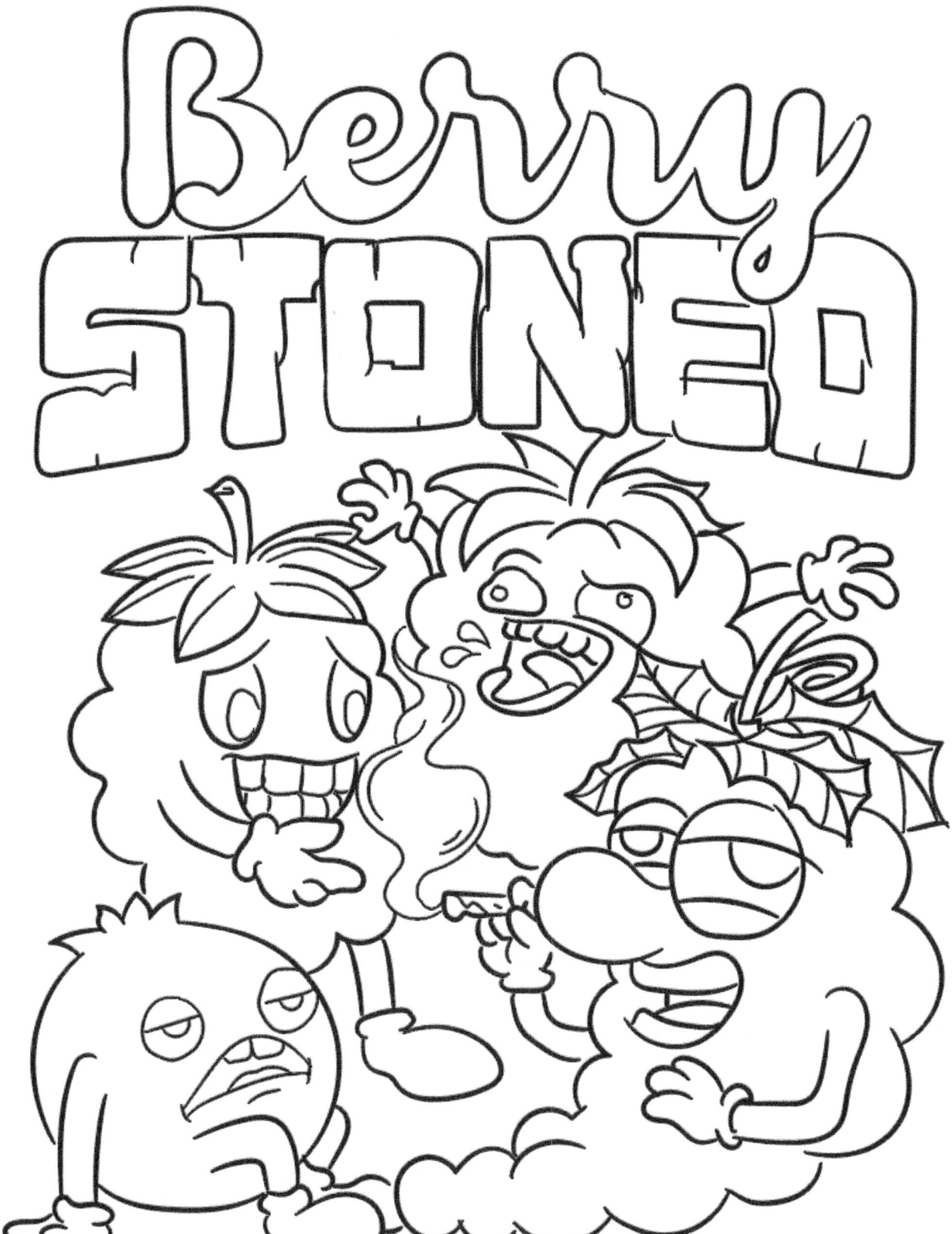
Berry
STONED

BAKE & CAKE

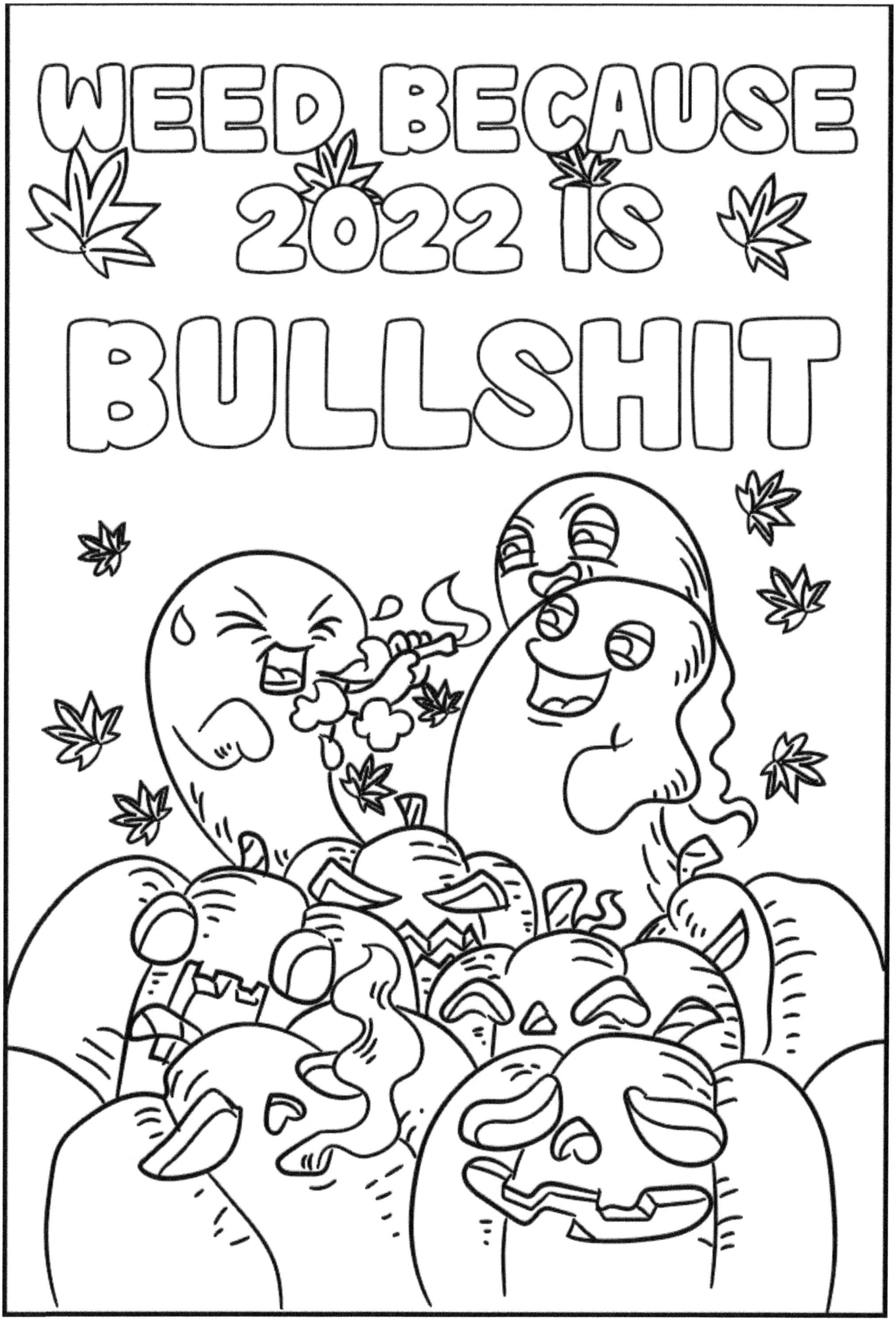
WEED BECAUSE 2022 IS
BULLSHIT

A WEE BIT

HIGHRISH

HOW WAS YOUR COLORING EXPERIENCE?

Let us know in a review on Amazon!
(Hint hint: We get so happy when we see photos and videos of your talented artist work! We'd be thrilled if you include a photo or video in your review)

Printed in Great Britain
by Amazon